IMAGES
*of America*

# NEWPORT

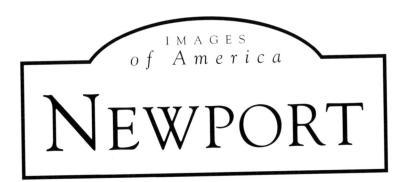

# IMAGES
# *of America*

# NEWPORT

Rob Lewis

ARCADIA

First printed in 1996.
Reprinted in 2000, 2002.

Published by Arcadia Publishing,
an imprint of Tempus Publishing, Inc.
2A Cumberland Street
Charleston, SC 29401

Printed in Great Britain.

For all general information contact Arcadia Publishing at:
Telephone 843-853-2070
Fax 843-853-0044
E-mail sales@arcadiapublishing.com

For customer service and orders:
Toll-Free 1-888-313-2665

Visit us on the internet at http://www.arcadiapublishing.com

The interior of Covell's hardware
store on Thames Street, c. 1880.

# Contents

Introduction 7

1. Thames Street 9

2. Washington Square and Vicinity 29

3. Docks and Wharves 41

4. Streets Around Town 53

5. The Point 63

6. Cliff Walk, Bellevue Avenue, and Ocean Drive 77

7. Newport Institutions 89

8. Beaches and Lighthouses 107

9. Streets Leaving Town 117

Acknowledgments 128

Newport Harbor looking southeast from the New England Steamship Company.

# Introduction

Newport was founded in 1639 by settlers looking for religious freedom. The proximity to the water was beneficial in many ways. It provided a natural harbor for commerce, and the ocean breezes kept the island cool in the summer and temperate in the winter months. Newport as a seaport thrived, and by the early 1700s it was larger than Boston. As late as 1769, Newport rivaled New York in foreign and domestic commerce. The Revolutionary War brought about an end to this, however. During the British occupation of Newport, over 480 structures were destroyed, and the seaport never regained its prominence.

The Fall River Line began its daily runs to Newport around 1847 and provided passage to Fall River, Boston, and New York—a service which lasted until 1937. Another lifeline to Newport was the Old Colony Railroad Company which began its service in 1863.

The mid to late 1800s are known to this day in Newport as "the Gilded Age." Artists and writers flocked to Newport each year for summer holidays. Luxurious hotels were built to accommodate the influx of summer residents, and by the late 1800s robber barons, industrial giants, and other wealthy folk began to build lavish estates—homes that were used as "summer cottages," for eight to twelve weeks each year.

In the 1950s and '60s, Newport was very much in jeopardy of losing many valuable relics of the past. The port was again dealt a devastating financial blow with the large-scale pullout of the navy. Coincidentally, in the late 1960s, tobacco heiress Doris Duke established the Newport Restoration Foundation, a non-profit organization whose mission was to preserve, protect, and restore the architecture of the eighteenth and early nineteenth centuries. Over eighty homes were purchased and restored, and eventually leased to private individuals. Today Newport has the most eighteenth-century homes of any city on the East Coast. Thanks to the efforts of "Operation Clapboard," the Newport Historical Society, the Newport Restoration Foundation, and many private restorations, the heritage of our past lives on!

# One
# Thames Street

New technology. An early photographer captures a moment in time on Thames Street at Washington Square. (Photograph from the *Daily News*, courtesy of the Newport Historical Society.)

Upper Thames Street. The John Steven's Shop, a family stone-cutting business, was founded in 1705 and has been on this spot since 1760.

The bow window from Feke's Apothecary Shop on Washington Square. In this photograph, the window has been moved to Dr. Johnson's store on Thames Street, between Marlborough Street and Washington Square. Today it is installed in the Newport Historical Society.

Upper Thames Street. The J.H. Barney and Co. piano store is shown here, *c.* 1906.

The parade grounds at the end of Thames Street. The building with bunting contained the Newport Business College.

Thames Street. In 1908 Thames
Street was paved with belgian
blocks—a durable surface that to
this day remains in some areas.
F.W. Woolworth is on the right.

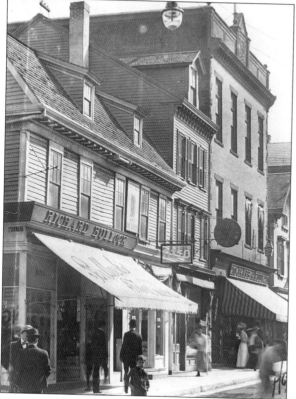

The corner of Mill and Thames
Streets. In the foreground is
Bullock's Shoe Store. The Music
Hall, erected c. 1894, is the tall
building in the background.

The west side of Thames Street opposite Church Street. Urban renewal forever replaced this block with America's Cup Avenue. The *Daily News* plant can be seen in the background. George Hermann's jewelry shop is in the foreground.

The corner of Green and Thames Street. The Kinsey Building was built to house the National Bank of Rhode Island. It is shown here with some of the construction crew, *c.* 1892. (Courtesy of the Newport Historical Society.)

The corner of Pelham and Thames Streets. The north side of this building was photographed after being damaged by hailstones, *c.* 1885. In 1805 Pelham was the first street in America to be lit by gas lights.

Thames Street at the corner of Cannon (Memorial Boulevard), *c.* 1884. The old customhouse can be seen in the distance.

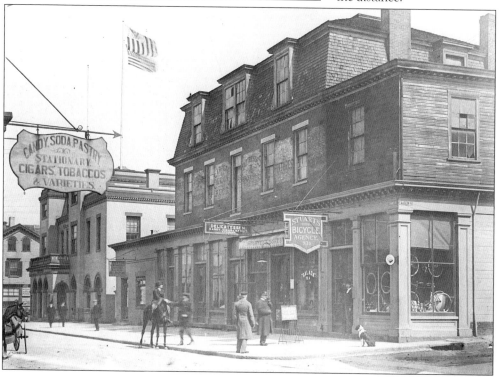

Thames Street near the corner of Swan Avenue. Someone had to keep the streets clean, and sweeping was the most efficient way to do so.

The east side of Thames at Gidley Street, *c.* 1894. Note the brick sidewalks—but the road is still dirt.

Thames Street. The political banner dominates this 1908 photograph.

Middle Thames Street around the turn of the century. The far store is the W.B. Sherman Dry Goods Co.

Franklin Street. This early photograph of the lower north side of Franklin Street was taken prior to 1880.

Thames Street at Franklin Street. The old customhouse was built in 1829 and demolished in 1916 to erect the current post office.

The north side of lower Franklin Street. This *c.* 1916 photograph was taken after the customhouse had been demolished in preparation for the new post office.

The south side of lower Franklin Street just prior to demolition. The doorway of the building in the left center of this image is now in the Museum of Newport History (Brick Market).

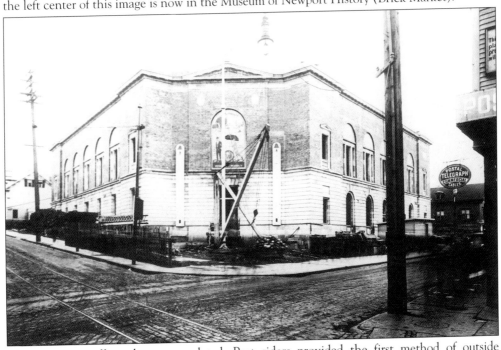

The new post office almost completed. Post riders provided the first method of outside communication. In 1716, a Newport to Boston stagecoach run began providing regular mail delivery.

The office of the Fall River Line. The steamship company began service in 1847 and provided daily excursions between Boston, Fall River, Newport, and New York. The luxury steamers continued until 1937 when the line went bankrupt.

Thames Street. This is a turn-of-the-century view, looking north from Cannon Street.

Armistice Day, 1934. This photograph was taken in front of the post office. (Courtesy of the Newport Historical Society.)

The Pinniger and Manchester Coal Co. This company operated from Perry Wharf from 1870 to the 1950s. The Perry Mill, the building with the tower, was constructed in 1835 to manufacture cotton and wool fabrics.

The Market Square Police Station. Built in 1867, it served as the police station until 1914, when a new station was built north of this one.

Market Square looking west from Thames Street. Albro's Fish Market can be seen to the right.

The south side of Market Square from Thames Street. Libby's Bakery, established in 1861, was at 9 Broadway. It is listed in the 1890 city directory.

Market Square at Thames Street. This photograph was taken looking east.

The police station in 1880.

The south side of Market Square behind the police station in 1880.

The rear of the Swinburne, Peckham and Co. building. It was torn down after 1900 to develop Government Landing (see p. 47).

The Francis Malbone House. Malbone came to Newport after 1700 and made a great fortune in the slave trade. Newport was a key point in the "triangle trade." Newport rum was shipped to Africa and traded for slaves. The slaves were taken to the Caribbean and exchanged for molasses. The molasses in turn was brought back to Newport to make rum and start the cycle again.

Lower Thames Street—the Samuel Whitehorne House. Whitehorne, a wealthy shipping merchant, started to build this house in 1811. With the decline of the slave trade and the War of 1812, he went bankrupt before it was completed. In this picture, taken around 1910, the building was home to Metropolitan Cleaners.

The Whitehorne House. The building was purchased by the Newport Restoration Foundation in 1968. It was restored and opened as a museum, and today it holds many fine examples of early Newport furniture.

Thames Street at the north end of Commercial Wharf. The southwest corner building housed the Holly Tree Coffee House.

*Two*

# Washington Square
# and Vicinity

Guizio Brangazio. "Joe the Peanut Man" sold peanuts at the north end of Washington Square.

The Colony House in 1860. This building was designed by Richard Munday and built in 1739. It sits at the top of the parade grounds, now known as Washington Square. The building was used as a barracks during the British occupation. During the French occupancy, it was used as a hospital, and during the eighteenth century, the basement was rented for shops.

The Spanish-American War memorial. In May 1899, a ceremonial archway was erected to commemorate Admiral William T. Sampson and his men, who fought in the Bay of Santiago—a key confrontation in the Spanish-American War.

A turn-of-the-century headline. The *Newport Daily News* headline on May 31, 1899 reads: "Newport's election celebration a complete success. Weather perfect, crowds immense and good-natured, decorations everywhere elaborate, parade an ovation to Sampson and his men . . ."

Election Day, May 30, 1899. Thousands of people crowded the streets for the noon inauguration of Elisha Dyer to a third term as governor.

Long Wharf and Brick Market. In 1760 the proprietors of Long Wharf set aside land for a market—the upper part to be used as stores for dry goods and the lower part as a market house. For ten years nothing was done, then Peter Harrison designed and built the Brick Market. Isaac Gould's house is to the left of Brick Market.

Brick Market. For a number of years the lower part of Brick Market was used as a market and watch house. From 1793 to 1799 it was rented as a theater. In 1842 the building was altered to serve as the town hall and it served as city hall from 1853 to 1900. It was restored in 1928. Today it is the Museum of Newport History run by the Newport Historical Society.

The area around the fountain. The town was originally set up around a natural spring at what is now Touro and Spring Streets. In 1802, the water was piped underground to Washington Square. In 1828, an ornamental cast-iron fountain was erected. The gambrel-roofed houses are the Charles Feke House (or the Pitts Head Tavern) and the adjoining 1796 Buttrick House (S.T. Buttrick, MD, is listed in the 1867 city directory). The Mumford House is also barely visible.

The parade grounds with a light dusting of snow. In 1799 it was renamed Washington Square. The present mall was laid out in 1800. Before the Revolutionary War, the town school and a print shop were located on a small street running through it.

Broadway at Farewell Street. This photograph was taken *c.* 1910, before the Army and Navy YMCA was built.

The YMCA. On November 9, 1910, the cornerstone-laying ceremony for the YMCA drew an impressive crowd. Senator George Peabody and Admiral S.B. Luce were among the dignitaries. Again, we see "Joe the Peanut Man" at work.

Building the Army and Navy YMCA, c. 1910–11.

The completed Army and Navy YMCA.

Washington Square, from the Army and Navy YMCA. This photograph shows the bandstand in the center of what is now Eisenhower Park. In the distance, the rectory for St. Joseph's School is visible.

The Pitts Head Tavern. This house was originally built around 1726 on the northwest corner of Charles and Queen Street (the area is now the north side of Washington Square). In 1765 Robert Lillibridge obtained the house and opened the Pitts Head Tavern, a coffee house. In 1877, the Independent Order of Odd Fellows purchased it and moved it to 5 Charles Street. Moved again in 1965, it is today located on Bridge Street. The roof line of the Hazard Memorial School building can be seen in the distance.

The Touro Synagogue on Touro Street around 1895. Built in 1763, this is the oldest synagogue in America. It closed during the Revolutionary War, but was reopened in 1883.

The Touro Synagogue. This is a close-up of the synagogue's gates.

The White Horse Tavern. Built in 1673 at the corner of Marlborough and Farewell Streets, it is the oldest operational tavern in the U.S. In this 1880 photograph, it was being operated by Mary Goodie as a boarding house.

The John Odlin House. Located at 41 Clarke Street, this building was built in 1750. Today it is the Melville House; restored, it serves as a bed and breakfast. The next house, at 31 Clarke Street, is the Robert Stevens House, which was built around 1709. During the French occupation, it was used as a barracks for Rochambeau's aides-de-camp.

The Newport Artillery Company, located on Clarke Street. The oldest military organization in the U.S. was chartered on February 1, 1741, by King George II. The armory was built in 1836. This photograph was taken c. 1890, before the 1907 fire. After the fire the armory was rebuilt and a second floor was added.

The corner of Clarke and Mary Streets. Part of the Vernon House was built prior to 1757. During the Revolutionary War it served as the headquarters for Count Rochambeau, and he met here with General Washington in March 1781.

Transportation for muddy streets. This sedan chair was found in the basement of the Vernon House in 1925.

# Three
# Docks and Wharves

Long Wharf. The Newport Water Works and some of its employees are shown here, *c.* 1884.

Long Wharf looking southeast. Many Newport shipwrights had their shops among the row of buildings to the left. In the 1863 town directory, eleven shipwrights are listed on Long Wharf.

Long Wharf at Washington Street, c. 1904. Prior to 1890, there was a drawbridge in the middle of Long Wharf to allow ships access to the cove. The bridge is on the Blaskowitz map of 1777.

The fire station. This station was located on the north side of Long Wharf in 1890.

Long Wharf. This mid-1800s view of Long Wharf from the city yard was originally a stereoscopic photograph.

Vessels at rest. The cat boats in this photograph, taken from south of Bowen's coal dock around 1885, look like they're resting peacefully.

The Anne Street Pier, viewed from the Newport Shipyard. The buildings in the distance are on Hammet's Wharf, where Christie's is located today.

The Benedict Arnold Jr. House. This building was erected around 1720 and demolished in 1925. It was located on Hammet's Wharf, now the site of Christie's.

Commercial Wharf around 1884. The Newport and Wickford Railroad and Steamship Co. had their Newport terminal located here. In this photograph, drivers and their hacks stand ready to pick up disembarking passengers.

The southwest corner of Champlin's Wharf. This wharf, built in the early 1800s, was owned by Christopher Champlin. It consisted of a two-story gable-roofed house on Thames Street and a small gambrel-roofed ell on the wharf side. Champlin traded with Sweden and St. Petersburg for iron and with Canton for silk and tea.

Government Landing. Built prior to World War I, Government Landing was used by government ferries transporting workers to and from the Goat Island Torpedo Station. This 1914 photograph shows a frozen harbor. Today, the Newport Harbor Hotel and Marina are located on this site.

The clutches of winter. This photograph was taken looking east-northeast from the Goat Island Torpedo Station, c. 1889. Luxury steamships from the Fall River Line can be seen across the ice-filled harbor (see p. 20).

The shot tower and lead works. Lead would be taken to the top of the tower and melted in a large pot. Once molten, it was poured through a hole in the floor, and as it fell to the bottom, it passed through screens which would break it into small pieces. From a cooling tank at the bottom, it was rolled into the plant to be made into lead shot and bullets. Built around 1857, the lead works ran around the clock during the Civil War.

The view northeast. St. Mary's Church, built in 1900, can be seen in the distance.

The view northwest. Overnight steamers from the Fall River Line can be seen docked at Long Wharf. In 1761, Ezra Stiles measured the wharfage in Newport and came up with 177,891 feet.

Looking east-northeast. The open area at the top of the photograph is the current site of the Newport Public Library. The King House can also be seen.

Looking southeast. Note the elms at the top of the photograph.

50

Looking northwest from the shot tower. A pod of navy ships is tied up in the harbor. In the distance is the Goat island Torpedo Station. Established in 1869, it continued operating until 1952. The officers' quarters, on the south end, were built in the 1870s.

Looking west from the tower toward Fort Adams. The original fortress was ordered to be built by George Washington and officially opened in 1799. The stone walls were added in 1824. Today the fort and its surroundings are maintained as a state park.

The shot lead works around 1916. The building had fallen into severe decay by this time and was demolished not too long after this photograph was taken.

An early submarine. Christened the *Holland*, this early sub is shown here in the harbor in the late 1890s.

# Four

# Streets Around Town

Gibbs Avenue, c. 1895. This was one of the smaller "summer cottages."

The junction of Spring Street and Broadway looking south around 1892. Spring Street was laid out in 1642. At that time it was known as the Back Street.

The corner of Barney and Spring Street. The building is the Jeffrey House; the First Baptist Church stands behind it.

Stone Street, looking east, with the Bull House in the background. This photograph shows a float from a parade in 1912.

The Henry Bull House located on Spring Street. This early photograph was taken around 1865. A rear portion of the house dates back to 1639—the year Newport was founded. Bull served as governor of Rhode Island from 1689 to 1690.

A turn-of-the-century photograph of the Bull House. The house was destroyed by fire in 1912.

The northeast corner of Touro and Spring Streets. This photograph was taken prior to 1922, when the building was raised up one floor to accommodate shops below. Today it is the home of Muriel's Restaurant.

The south side of Mary Street just below Spring. The David Cheseborough House was built in 1737. In 1908, it was torn down to build the YMCA, which is still standing today.

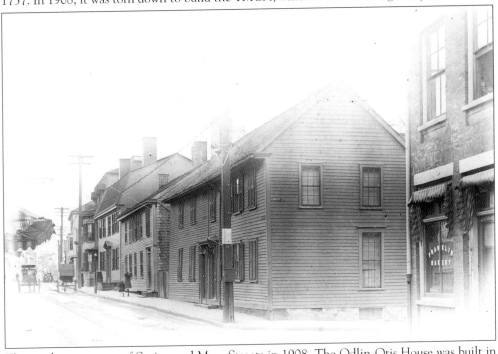

The southwest corner of Spring and Mary Streets in 1908. The Odlin-Otis House was built in 1705. During the 1780s it served as a Quaker school for boys. The Franklin Bakery can be seen in the foreground.

The John Bannister House, built c. 1751. Bannister was a prominent Newport sea merchant and land owner. Between 1776 and 1779, General Richard Prescott made his headquarters here. During the summer of 1777, the weather was oppressively hot and he moved his headquarters to the Nichols-Overing House on the Kings Highway, now West Main Road in Portsmouth. On the night of July 9, 1777, Colonel William Barton and a group of men crossed the bay from Warwick Neck and were successful in capturing General Prescott in the middle of the night. This is a c. 1865 photograph.

The Bannister House around 1905. Note the trolley line passing the house.

The southwest corner of Spring and Pelham Streets. The small gambrel-roofed house, built in 1771, was used as a guard house by Hessian soldiers guarding General Prescott.

Cannon Street. This *c.* 1912 view is of the north side looking west.

Levin Street near Spring at the rear of St. Mary's Church. St. Mary's is where Jacqueline Bouvier married John Fitzgerald Kennedy in 1953. The building was erected in 1848.

The fire station on Marlborough Street. This photograph was taken after a storm toppled the station's hose tower.

The Governor William Wanton House, built prior to 1740. This 1900s photograph shows the first floor as a storefront. William Wanton served as governor from 1732 to 1734.

The Judge Joslin House, located at the lower end of Pelham Street. Stewart's Livery Stable and One Pelham East can be seen past the judge's house.

Senaca Sprague on the parade (see p. 92).

*Five*

# The Point

The Basin in 1887. After the railroad laid its tracks to Long Wharf the Basin was divided in two, and in 1891 the west half was filled with 10,000 train-car loads of dirt.

The Basin prior to 1890. This photograph was taken from the far end of Long Wharf looking northeast.

Looking southwest from the old fire station tower at the foot of Marlborough Street. The Fall River Line steamship *Massachusetts* can be seen docked at the end of Long Wharf in this c. 1880 photograph.

Marsh Street, c. 1920. Thirty years earlier the north side of the street bordered on the Basin.

The north end of the cove along Bridge Street, prior to 1890. The east end of Bridge Street was originally called Shipwright Street.

The Bridge Street Fire Station, c. 1880. This building housed Steam Engine No. 2 "rough and ready." In 1880, sixteen fire alarm boxes were listed in the city directory.

The Captain Peter Simon House. The early part of this house dates to 1727, and in the mid-1700s Simon enlarged it. The house was restored through "Operation Clapboard" and is a private residence today. Located on the north side of Bridge Street, it is shown here in a view looking east from the railroad tracks.

Third Street at the corner of Bridge Street. The house to the right is the Thomas Townsend House, which was built *c.* 1735. Thomas Townsend was an innkeeper. He purchased the house in 1795.

Third Street at the corner of Bridge Street. This photograph shows the same intersection a few years later after a snowstorm. The house on the left is the Martha Pitman House, which was built in the mid to late 1700s.

Bridge Street in 1880. The second house on the right is the Caleb Claggett House. The next house down is 16 Bridge Street, the home of his son William Claggett, the well-known organ and clock maker.

The Caleb Claggett House at 22 Bridge Street, built in 1725. The "s" braces on the sides are not only ornamental, but keep the ends from bowing out under the weight of the house.

The John Goddard House at 81 Second Street. The house and shop were originally built on Washington Street on the site of the Covell House, but around 1869 they were moved to Second Street near Pine Street. Goddard was a well-known cabinetmaker and his work is very sought after.

Goddard's workshop on Smith Court off Poplar Street. This building was demolished in the late 1950s. It is shown here pre-1930.

The Franklin Weaver House. This one-and-a-half-story residence was located on Walnut Street at Second Street.

The Caswell House at 14 Third Street. The house was built *c.* 1767. Philip Caswell purchased it in 1854.

The southwest corner of Walnut and Third Streets. Although it has been through many renovations, the original roof line can still be seen. Today it is the home of the Walnut Street Market.

The Poplar Street ramp at Washington Street. The house to the right is the Captain John Warren House, which was built prior to 1749. The gambrel-roofed house to the left is the Thomas Robinson House. Built around 1725, it was the headquarters of the Vicomte de Noailles during the Revolutionary War. Very few changes have been made to either house through the years.

The gambrel-roofed Dye-Carr House, *c.* 1740. The next house is 54 Poplar Street—the Jonathan Chadwick House, built *c.* 1725.

The John Dennis House. Built *c.* 1740, this building is located at 65 Poplar and Washington Streets. The portico that was added in the late 1800s can be seen in this 1890 photograph. It was removed during a later restoration.

Battling a fire. This blaze occurred at 37 Poplar Street on September 28, 1929.

The "Liberty Tree" at Poplar and Thames Streets. The first tree was planted in 1766. Today the tree that grows on this site is the fourth to bear that title.

The Elm Street Pier in the late 1890s.

A view north from Elm Street in the late 1800s. Rail service was begun in Newport in 1863 by the Old Colony Railroad Company.

The east side of the Basin in the mid-1870s. This area was filled in after 1900, and is the present site of Cardine's Field.

The harbor from Washington Street, c. 1885. The ship in the distance is the USS *Constellation*.

An old Newport hose wagon on the Point. The Van Zandt Pier can be seen in the background.

A steam-powered fire pumper on Washington Street. The first steam-powered fire engine was purchased by the city in 1806. In 1888, there were 124 firemen listed on the city coffers.

# Six
# Cliff Walk,
# Bellevue Avenue,
# and Ocean Drive

Ocean Drive. This photograph was taken near Green Bridge around the turn of the century.

Bath Road, showing the start of Cliff Walk.

Forty Steps is located on Cliff Walk. It allows safe access to the surf below.

Forty Steps, *c*. 1895.

Summer cottages along Cliff Walk, *c*. 1885. Land owners have tried many times to block passage along the cliffs, but the courts have always upheld water-access rights.

A tunnel on Cliff Walk.

Ochre Point along Cliff Walk. Ochre Point was purchased in 1844 for the sum of $14,000 by William Lawrence. Several years later he sold parts of the property to friends—a decision he later regretted.

"The Breakers." The most splendid and opulent of Newport's summer cottages is shown here in 1948. The mansion, built by Cornelius Vanderbilt and designed by Richard Morris Hunt, took three years to build and was completed in 1895. The house has seventy rooms and was used for about two months out of every year. Today, it is owned by the Preservation Society of Newport and is maintained as a museum.

"The Breakwater." More commonly known as Lippett's Castle, this structure was built in 1899 at the end of Ledge Road by Charles Lippett, who made his fortune from the cotton industry. Lippett was also governor of Rhode Island from 1895 to 1897. The castle was demolished in 1925 to build a residence for architect John Russell Pope.

A boathouse and local fishermen at the foot of Ledge Road.

The end of Bellevue Avenue where it meets Touro Street. This house sits on the site where the Hotel Viking was erected in the 1920s.

Abraham's Block, located on the west side of Bellevue Avenue between Levin and William Streets. This is a c. 1890 photograph.

The Stone Mill in Touro Park. This photograph of the mill was taken in 1860. The exact date and reason for the structure continues to elude scholars today.

The Traver's Block at the corner of Bellevue Avenue and Bath Road (now Memorial Boulevard). Built in 1875, it soon became the shopping area for wealthy summer colonists, c. 1900.

The Newport Casino. The casino was built in 1880 by J. Gordon Bennett Jr. and designed by architect Stanford White. This photograph was taken in the courtyard around 1890.

Sleighing down Bellevue Avenue in front of the casino.

The corner of Bellevue Avenue and Deblois Street. This structure is the Kazanjian Building, built c. 1890s.

Bellevue Avenue. On April 8, 1875, the anniversary parade of the Newport Transfer Co.—the "original Burtons Express"—marched down Bellevue Avenue.

The Ocean House. This was the premier hotel to stay at in the early part of the 1840s. On August 3, 1845, it was destroyed by fire. Rebuilt shortly after the fire, this view shows the hotel as it appeared in the 1880s. In September 1898, a second fire destroyed it, and it was never rebuilt.

The gatehouse for Ochre Court, c. 1890. Today it is part of the campus of Salve Regina University.

## *Seven*
# Newport Institutions

The Redwood Library. Located on Bellevue Avenue, the library was founded in 1748. The land was donated by Henry Collins and the building designed by Peter Harrison. The Redwood Library has the honor of being the oldest library in America. In 1880, it had 22,566 books in its inventory.

Duke Street at Washington Square. This building was built before 1722. In 1793, Abraham Rodrigues Rivera, a wealthy merchant, purchased the house. In 1803 the Newport National Bank was established and still maintains a bank here.

The White House Lunch Wagon.

The Newport Historical Society—founded in 1853 and incorporated in 1854. The Sabbatarian Order disbanded in 1835; in 1885 the Sabbatarian meetinghouse was placed in the care of the Newport Historical Society and moved from Barney Street to Touro Street, adjoining the society.

F.W.S. Sprague in 1888.

F.W.S. Sprague. Sprague preached to crowds that George Washington was the second Messiah.

Washington Square in the 1880s. The Opera House to the left seated one thousand people. To rent it for a night cost $50, including ushers and ticket-takers. The adjoining Perry House Hotel was listed in city directories from the 1880s through the turn of the century.

Clarke Street. This building originally served as the Second Congregational Church in 1847, and then became the Central Baptist Church. The church is shown here in 1885. Washington Square can be seen in the distance.

St Paul's Methodist Church. This church was built on Marlborough Street in 1806.

The North Baptist Church. Designed by Russell Warren in 1834, it was torn down in 1906. The old burying ground lies to the south of the church.

The Trinity Church schoolhouse.
This building, built in 1799, was
located at the corner of Mary
Street at 25 School Street.

The Channing Memorial Church
on Pelham Street. Founded by Dr.
William E. Channing in 1835, this
edifice was built in 1881.

The *Newport*. Ferry service between Newport and Jamestown began around 1679. Ferries were powered by sail until the mid-1870s, when the steam-powered ferry made its debut. The *Newport* made its last run in 1969 when the Newport Bridge opened. From here it went to Pawtucket's old State Pier and served as a youth center until 1974. It is now a floating restaurant in Portland, Maine.

Coaster's Harbor Island. In 1819 the Newport Asylum was erected here to care for the infirm and poor. It was closed in 1884. In 1885, Commodore S.B. Luce opened the Naval War College here after extensive renovations.

The view aboard the deck of the USS *Constellation*.

A full view of the ship docked in the harbor.

Built on Coaster's Harbor Island in 1891–92, this became the new home of the Naval War College. Today it is named Luce Hall after the founder of the college (see p. 96).

The Civil War Monument. This monument was erected by Charles E. Lawton and the citizens of Newport in 1890. The First Presbyterian Church, built in 1890–92, lies nearly finished in the background.

The dirigible *Shenandoah*. In August 1924, during trials to increase the use of airships during war time, the *Shenandoah* successfully attached itself to the mooring mast of the USS *Patoka*.

The arrival of the circus. A circus tent is shown here being raised at Festival Field on the outskirts of town.

The circus train. Native Americans are shown here unloading horses from the train of a visiting circus.

Trinity Church. This was one of the first structures designed by Richard Munday. The original church dates back to 1702, and in 1726, Munday was hired to enlarge it. The grand spire, modeled after the one on Christ Church in Boston, was added in the 1740s. This is the oldest Episcopal parish in New England.

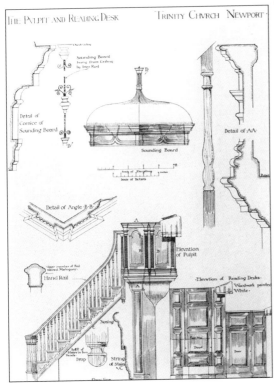

Detailed drawings of Trinity's moldings and its unusual wine-glass pulpit.

The Newport Hospital, founded in 1873. For $4,800, Henry Ledyard purchased a piece of land, almost an acre in size, to be used as the site of the hospital. The location was chosen because "it was on high ground, away from the thickly settled part of the city, commanding a full view of the sea, and exposed to its healthy breezes." The Ledyard Ward, to the left, was built in 1873. To the right is the Littlefield Ward, an 1893 addition. (All photographs of the hospital were provided by Helen E. Jones; they are *Daily News* photographs and used with the permission of the Newport Historical Society.)

The Contagion Ward, built in 1903.

The 1892 graduates of the Newport Hospital School of Nursing. The 1892 city directory lists forty-nine nurses as providers of care to the city.

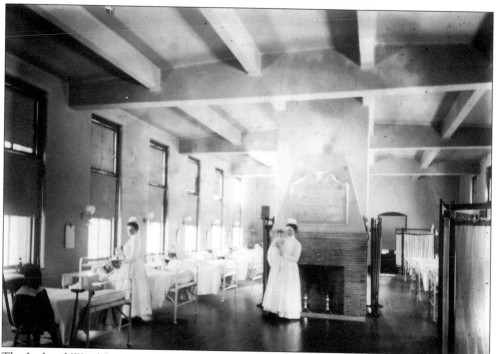

The Ledyard Ward for women in 1903.

Hospital buildings. This photograph was taken after 1903 when the Vanderbilt Pavilion, on the left, was built. On the right is the Hazard Building, which was also added in 1903, and in the far middle is the School of Nursing building. The Turner Building, erected in 1968, now blocks this view.

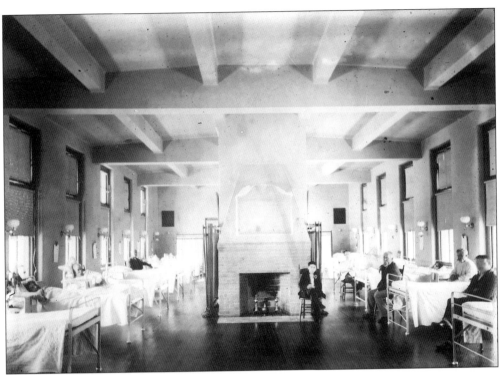

The Littlefield Ward for men in 1903.

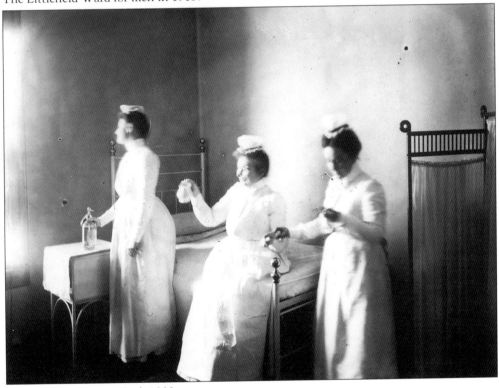

Nurses in the Carey Ward, 1903.

The graduating class of 1896.

Ley's Century Store. This 1954 photograph shows a nursing recruitment display in the window.

*Eight*

# Beaches and Lighthouses

Easton's Beach. A cozy cab surrey leaves Easton's Beach in the late 1800s.

An early stereoscopic picture of Easton's Beach.

The ice house on Easton's Pond. This early picture shows Easton's Pond prior to the beach's build up.

Dressed for the beach in 1890. The pavilion and bath houses are to the left. Trolley service had already reached the beach.

Bath Road looking south towards Easton's Beach in 1889. In the distance very few houses can be seen on the esplanade.

Easton's Beach, c. 1890.

Bathers at the water's edge around 1900.

Transportation on Easton's Beach. Horse-drawn carriages were once a common site on the beach, but with the invention of the automobile, car races up and down the beach became popular.

King's Park Beach, *c.* 1860. The Lime Rock Lighthouse and Fort Adams can be seen in the distance.

Bailey's Beach. Sometime around 1850, the land which is now Bailey's Beach was purchased by Joseph Bailey. For a $100 fee, the wealthy were allowed access to the beach and the right to build a small cabana or have a beach car. This photograph shows the beach prior to the Hurricane of 1938.

Bailey's Beach. In 1897 the beach was incorporated. The Spouting Rock Beach Association was named after a turret of water which spouted through a natural rock formation. At half tide, the water spout would shoot up to 50 feet into the air.

Bailey's Beach, rebuilt, sometime after 1938.

The Goat Island Lighthouse around 1900. The first lighthouse on this spot was built in 1824. In 1842, it was replaced by this structure.

The Lime Rock Lighthouse. This lighthouse was later renamed after Ida Lewis, who tended the light for many years in the mid-1800s. During her tenure as lighthouse keeper, she is credited with saving at least eighteen lives. In the 1870s she was awarded the Medal of Congress—the first woman to receive this honor.

The Rose Island Lighthouse. Built on the site of an eighteenth-century fort, the Rose Island Lighthouse was lit in 1870. In 1971, the building was abandoned, but in 1984 the Rose Island Lighthouse Foundation was established to rescue it. Today it has been restored, relit, and is open for tours. You can also make arrangements to stay overnight as a guest in the lighthouse.

The Gull Rock Lighthouse in the 1890s.

The Sandy Point Light on Prudence Island around 1890. Originally, this light was built in 1824 on the north end of Goat Island, but in 1851 it was moved to its present site. It is still in operation (see p. 114).

The lighthouse at Castle Hill.

# *Nine*
# Streets Leaving Town

One Mile Corner, *c.* 1890, looking north.

The second asylum. After the Poor Asylum was closed on Coaster's Harbor Island, the poor and indigent were housed in this building on Broadway after 1885 (see p. 96).

Broadway at Bliss Road, c. 1915. For many years a gas station stood on the empty lot to the right. Today it is the site of Frasch's Bakery (established in 1865).

The J.A. Leary and Sons General Store, *c*. 1917, located on Broadway near Equality Park.

Broadway opposite Mann Avenue. The gentleman walking across the street is believed to be Senaca Sprague (see p. 92).

City Hall Square. This nighttime shot casts an eerie glow in City Hall Square around 1912. The light-colored building in the center is the Smith Block, which had been destroyed by a fire in September 1911. It is shown here, with its new facade, after being rebuilt.

Horseless carriages. This *c.* 1913 photograph shows a line of Chase automobiles in front of the Tisdall and Co. grocery store. The building, built in 1900, is currently home to Newport Hardware. (Photograph from the *Daily News*, courtesy of the Newport Historical Society.)

Broad Street (now Broadway), looking north from Bull Street in the mid-1800s.

A view from Bull Street looking south down Broad Street, again in the mid-1800s. To the right is Marlborough Street, which originally extended to the harbor. The Marlborough Street Wharf was the first wharf built in Newport.

The Townsend Industrial School, built in 1893. This photograph was taken prior to 1905, when the high school was built to the left, and after 1900, when the city hall was built to the right.

Newport's second high school, located on Broadway. Roger's High School was dedicated in 1874 and located on School Street at the corner of Church Street. The second building to house the high school was built on Broadway in 1905. In March 1920, it was gutted by fire and took a year to rebuild. In 1957, the high school was moved to Wickham Road and the building on Broadway became Thompson Junior High.

The Wanton-Lyman-Hazard House at 17 Broadway. Stephen Mumford built this building around 1675, making it Newport's oldest house. The roof line is kicked-out to provide a wide overhang, also known as a witches' bonnet. The house was purchased in 1927 by the Newport Historical Society and restored in the same year. Today it is open seasonally for guided tours. (Courtesy of the Newport Historical Society.)

The first George Weaver Hardware Store at 19 Broadway. Shortly after this fire, he rebuilt and expanded into 23 Broadway.

The second George Weaver Hardware Store. Sadly, the second store was also destroyed by fire. The presence of the city hall tower in the background tells us that this photograph was taken after 1900.

A mobile Newport residence. Around 1900 this house was moved from Broadway to West Broadway. Moving entire houses was once much more common then it is today.

The top of Levin Street. The middle house of this section of houses was slated for the wrecker's ball. The house to the left is Cappy's Tavern.

Bath Road, *c.* 1921, covered with snow and ice.

Bath Road showing the trolley line to Easton's Beach. This first line was opened in August 1889 and eventually expanded to include other outlying areas of the city. Fares were 5¢ one way.

Bath Road. This photograph of the top of Bath Road, looking east toward Easton's Beach, was taken after 1895.

I leave you with a fitting photograph for the end of the book: Farewell Street, as it passes the North Baptist Church, prior to 1900.

# Acknowledgments

The first of my acknowledgments must go to Benjamin C. Reed Jr., the executive director of the Newport Restoration Foundation. For over twenty years he has guided the foundation through the procurement, restoration, and preservation of some of Newport's most precious gifts—her eighteenth and early nineteenth-century homes. Through his generosity, Ben has allowed me to peruse the Newport Restoration Foundation's photographic archives and to amass a collection of Newport photographs from the 1860s through the turn of the century.

Many people held my hand and gave me direction when I was at a road block. M. Joan Youngken, the deputy director for collections at the Newport Historical Society, was very supportive with help and information. Helen Jones, the former director of the Newport Hospital School of Nursing, provided the wonderful photographs of the hospital in chapter 7. Thanks to Charlotte Johnson, the executive director of the Rose Island Lighthouse Foundation, for her keen insight on the bay; to Mary Jackson and Pat Dennett, for knowledge only Newporters could provide; to Bob Lennon, who kept everything else going when this project consumed me; and to the photographers of the past—J.A. Williams, P. Caswell, W.E. Warren, M. Hall, W. Covell, S. Kerschner, J. Bergner, and others—who were the original preservers of Newport. And a special thank you to Mary Ellen O'neil, Meo, for her help at the end.